Looking at Science
How Things Change

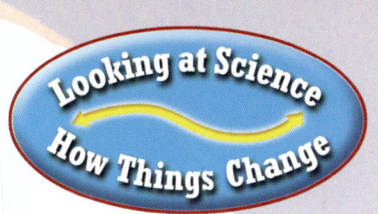

Looking at Solids, Liquids, and Gases

How Does Matter Change?

Jackie Gaff

Enslow Elementary
an imprint of
Enslow Publishers, Inc.
40 Industrial Road
Box 398
Berkeley Heights, NJ 07922
USA
http://www.enslow.com

Enslow Elementary, an imprint of Enslow Publishers, Inc.

Enslow Elementary® is a registered trademark of Enslow Publishers, Inc.

This edition published in 2008 by Enslow Publishers, Inc.

Copyright © 2008 The Brown Reference Group plc

All rights reserved.

No part of this book may be reproduced by any means without the written permission of the publisher.

Library of Congress Cataloging-in-Publication Data

Gaff, Jackie.
  Looking at solids, liquids, and gases : how does matter change? / Jackie Gaff
     p. cm. — (Looking at science : how things change)
  Summary: "Provides an introduction for readers on the differences between the states of matter"—Provided by publisher.
  Includes bibliographical references and index.
  ISBN-13: 978-0-7660-3092-3
  ISBN-10: 0-7660-3092-X
  1. Matter—Properties—Juvenile literature. I. Title.
  QC173.36.G35 2008
  530.4—dc22

2007024514

Printed in the United States of America

10 9 8 7 6 5 4 3 2 1

To Our Readers: We have done our best to make sure all Internet Addresses in this book were active and appropriate when we went to press. However, the author and the publisher have no control over and assume no liability for the material available on those Internet sites or on other Web sites they may link to. Any comments or suggestions can be sent by e-mail to comments@enslow.com or to the address on the back cover.

Every effort has been made to locate all copyright holders of material used in this book. If any errors or omissions have occurred, corrections will be made in future editions of this book.

For The Brown Reference Group plc
Project Editor: Sarah Eason
Designer: Paul Myerscough
Picture Researcher: Maria Joannou
Children's Publisher: Anne O'Daly

Photo and Illustration Credits: The Brown Reference Group plc (illustrations), pp. 21T, 21B, 26; Dreamstime, p. 17T; istockphoto, pp. 2, 4, 4B, 5B, 6, 8B (x3), 9T, 10, 13T, 13B, 14B (x2), 16, 18, 22, 22B, 24, 25T, 26, 28, 29B, 30; Paul Myerscough, p. 24B; Photos.com, 11, 12B, 20B; Shutterstock, pp. 1, 7B, 8, 12, 14, 16B, 20, 23T. NASA, p. 27T; Geoff Ward (illustrations), pp. 18, 19.
Cover Photo: Shutterstock

Contents

What is matter? 4
What are solids, liquids, and gases? 6
What are solids like? 8
What are liquids like? 10
What are gases like? 12
How much does matter weigh? 14
Can matter change? 16
What is matter made of? 18
How does heat change solids? 20
How do liquids change into gases? 22
How do gases change into liquids? 24
Why is water so important? 26
What do I know about matter? 28
Words to Know 30
Learn More 31
Index 32

What is matter?

Everything is made of matter. The home you live in is made of matter. The clothes you wear are made of matter. The food you eat and the air you breathe are made of matter.

bricks

wood

concrete

Even your body is made of matter!

▶ About two thirds of the matter in your body is water.

◀ This house is made of matter, such as concrete, wood, and bricks.

What are solids, liquids, and gases?

Matter has different states, or forms. Solids are one state of matter. Liquids are another state of matter. Gases are a third state of matter.

▼ What states of matter can be seen in this picture?

The wood in a tree is solid.

The air we breathe is made of gases.

Solid rock can be found on a mountain.

Solids, liquids, and gases behave in different ways. That is how you can tell them apart.

▲ Gases are moving this kite. You cannot see the gases in air, but you can see them at work when the wind blows.

The water in this lake is liquid.

7

What are solids like?

A solid has a particular shape and size. It does not change shape easily.

▼ These objects are solid. Their sizes and shapes do not change easily.

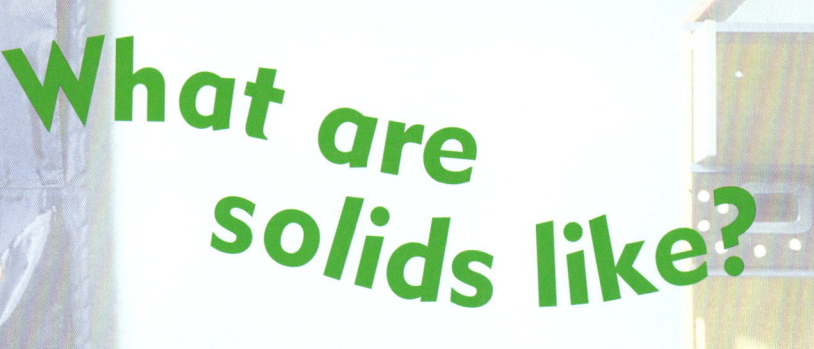

▲ Even a tiny solid, such as a grain of sand, has its own shape.

You can pick up a solid and turn it around. Its shape will stay the same.

What are liquids like?

Unlike solids, liquids easily change shape. When you pour liquid from a bottle into a cup, it changes from the shape of the bottle to the shape of the cup.

◀ A liquid takes the shape of its container.

◄ Unlike solids, liquids flow. That is why it is hard to pick up a liquid without a container.

Unlike a solid, a liquid does not have a particular shape of its own.

11

What are gases like?

Gases do not have a particular shape or size. Gases spread out to fill the space or container they are in.

Gases can also be forced to fit into smaller spaces.

◄ If gases are not contained, they spread outward. That is why you have to tie a knot in a balloon.

Usually gases cannot ▶ be seen or touched. Some gases do have a smell, though. A gas called hydrogen sulfide smells like rotten eggs!

▲ Air is a mixture of gases. This balloon had air in it, but was not tied. The air spread out of the balloon and into air outside.

How much does matter weigh?

Two objects may be the same size. But one may weigh more than the other. The heavier one has more matter in the same amount of space. It has more density.

▲ A rock weighs more than a bar of soap of the same size. That is because the rock has more density than the soap.

A gallon of water and a gallon of oil are the same size. But the gallon of water is heavier than the gallon of oil. That is because the water contains more matter than the oil in the same amount of space. It has more density.

◀ An iceberg floats because ice has less density than water. Ice contains less matter than the same amount of water.

Can matter change?

Matter can change in different ways. For example, it can change state.

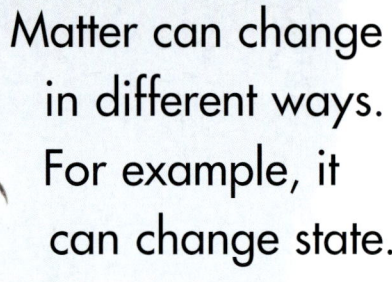

◀ If you freeze juice, it turns from a liquid into a solid. This popsicle is made of juice (a liquid) that has been frozen into ice (a solid).

▶ These icicles are changing from solid ice back into liquid water.

Water changes state when it is boiled. It turns from a liquid to a gas called water vapor.

When water is frozen, it changes state and becomes solid ice.

But water is still water, whether it is a solid, a liquid, or a gas.

What is matter made of?

All matter is made of tiny moving pieces that cannot be seen. They are called atoms and molecules. The atoms and molecules of solids, liquids, and gases all move differently.

Solid molecules are held together by strong bonds. That stops the molecules from moving around.

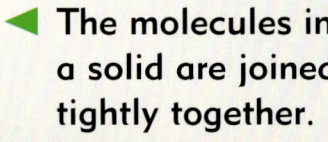
◀ The molecules in a solid are joined tightly together.

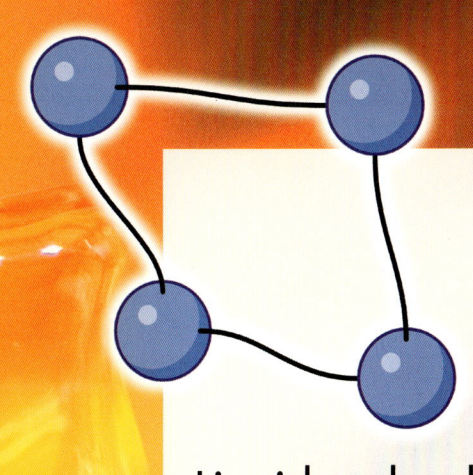

◀ The molecules in a liquid are joined loosely together. Liquid molecules can move around.

Liquid molecules are held together by loose bonds. That allows the molecules to move.

Gas molecules are not held together by any bonds. They move freely.

The molecules ▶ in a gas are not joined together at all. They move very quickly.

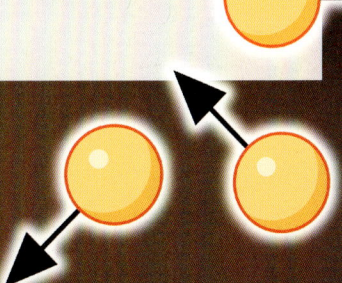

19

How does heat change solids?

Heat is a form of energy. When a solid is heated, the heat energy makes the molecules move around more. This makes the solid melt into a liquid.

▼ Heat from the warm corn makes the solid butter melt into liquid!

lava

Even solid rock ▶ will melt if it becomes very hot. Lava is liquid rock that pours from a volcano when it erupts.

If the liquid cools down, it becomes solid again.

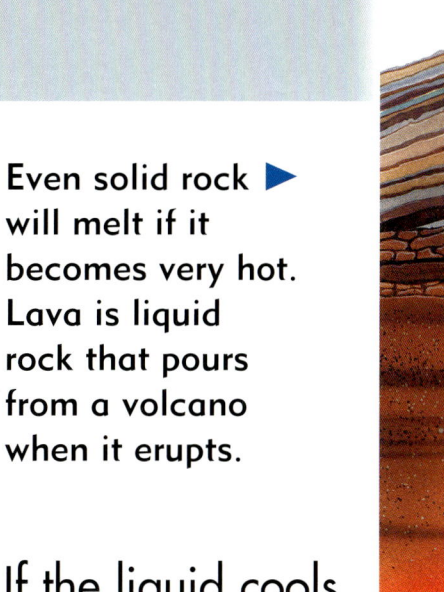

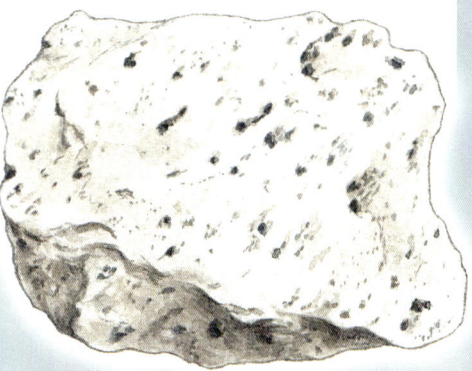

▲ Lava turns back into solid rock when it cools down again.

How do liquids change into gases?

When a liquid is heated, molecules at the surface move around quickly and escape into the air as a gas. That is why puddles dry up when the Sun shines.

The change from a liquid into a gas is called evaporation.

▶ The hot water in this tea kettle is evaporating as water vapor, or steam.

How do gases change into liquids?

Do you know why the bathroom mirror mists up when you take a hot shower or bath? When the warm water vapor (a gas) hits the cooler mirror, the water vapor cools. That makes it change back into liquid water. The mist you see is made of tiny water droplets.

24

▲ Tiny water droplets join inside a rain cloud to make bigger water droplets. When the droplets become big and heavy, they fall as rain.

The change from a gas to a liquid is called condensation.

Why is water so important?

Water is Earth's most precious matter. About two thirds of Earth's surface is water. All living things need water to stay alive.

The Water Cycle

1 The Sun's heat makes water evaporate from rivers, lakes, and oceans. Water also evaporates from plants and the soil.

2 Water vapor rises into the air. As it cools, it condenses into droplets of liquid water. The droplets form clouds.

3 Water falls from the clouds as rain. It can also freeze into snow or ice.

Earth is the only planet known to have both liquid water and living things.

Water is always moving and changing. It falls as rain or snow. It flows into rivers and oceans. It freezes into ice in winter, then melts in the spring.

Water changes from a liquid to a gas that floats up into the air. Water then changes from a gas to a liquid, and falls back to Earth as rain. We call this the water cycle.

What do I know about matter?

1. Try changing water from a liquid into a solid or a gas!
   - Shake a bottle of water. The water moves because it is a liquid.
   - Freeze the bottle overnight. Now what happens to the bottle when you shake it? The water is solid ice.
   - Put the bottle out into the sunlight with the lid off. The water level should go down as the warmth makes the water evaporate into a gas.

2. When you take a hot shower or bath, look for the mist of water droplets on the mirror. Can you remember how they are made?

3. Shake a rock. Turn it around. Can you remember why it does not change shape? Now pour some milk into a glass. Did it change shape? Why?

4. Leave an ice cube out in a small bowl. How does it change shape in the bowl? What does it change into?

Words to Know

atom — The smallest part of matter.

condensation — When a gas changes into a liquid.

density — How much matter something has compared to its size. Different things can be the same size, but have different densities.

evaporation — When a liquid changes into a gas.

lava — Hot liquid rock that flows from volcanoes.

matter — Everything that exists. Matter is made up of different kinds of atoms and molecules.

molecule — A very small part of matter. Molecules are made of atoms.

states — Three states or forms of matter are solids, liquids, and gases.

water vapor — A gas. When water evaporates it changes into water vapor.

Learn More

Books

Garrett, Ginger. *Solids, Liquids, and Gases.* San Francisco: Children's Press (2005).

Glover, David. *Solids and Liquids.* Boston: Kingfisher (2002).

Ontario Science Centre. *Solids, Liquids and Gases.* New York: Kids Can Press (2005).

Web Sites

Rader's Chem4Kids
www.chem4kids.com

Strange Matter
www.strangematterexhibit.com

Index

A
atom, 18

C
condensation, 25

D
density, 14–15

E
Earth, 26–27
energy, 20
evaporation, 23

G
gas, 6–7, 12–13, 17, 18–19, 22–23, 24–25, 26–27

H
heat, 20–21, 22, 26

I
ice, 15, 16–17, 26–27

L
liquid, 6–7, 10–11, 16–17, 18–19, 20–21, 22–23, 24–25, 26–27

M
molecules, 18–19, 20, 22

R
rain, 25, 26–27

S
snow, 27
solid, 6–7, 8–9, 10–11, 16–17, 18, 20–21
states of matter, 6, 16–17

W
water, 7, 14–15, 17, 23, 24–25, 26–27
water cycle, 27
water vapor, 17, 23, 24, 26